Tastes from the regions of Italy

Travelling around Italy you'll find that the regional cuisine is drawn from those ingredients that are available in abundance locally. These regional dishes pair wonderfully with local wines and even olive oil from the region. Robust and peppery extra virgin olive oils from Tuscany are delicious drizzled on hearty Tuscan soups such as Zuppa di Farro (page 7).

At the heart of Italian cooking are the principles of simplicity, and eating with the seasons using ···ipe booklet ···ollection of

D0807457

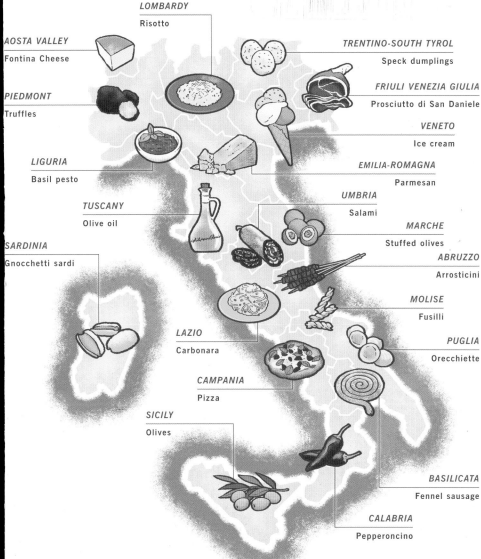

LOMBARDY
Risotto

AOSTA VALLEY
Fontina Cheese

TRENTINO-SOUTH TYROL
Speck dumplings

PIEDMONT
Truffles

FRIULI VENEZIA GIULIA
Prosciutto di San Daniele

VENETO
Ice cream

LIGURIA
Basil pesto

EMILIA-ROMAGNA
Parmesan

UMBRIA
Salami

TUSCANY
Olive oil

MARCHE
Stuffed olives

SARDINIA
Gnocchetti sardi

ABRUZZO
Arrosticini

MOLISE
Fusilli

LAZIO
Carbonara

PUGLIA
Orecchiette

CAMPANIA
Pizza

SICILY
Olives

BASILICATA
Fennel sausage

CALABRIA
Pepperoncino

3

Baccalà mantecato

Baccalà mantecato is a fluffy, white cloud of salt cod that is soaked and prepared like a sauce. An iconic appetiser from Venice, you'll find this delicious snack in the city's *cicchetti* (the Venetian word for small snacks) bars, which are also known as *bàcari*.

Serves 8 as an appetizer

Prep: 10 minutes plus 24 hours soaking time
Cook: 10 minutes

400g	salt cod fillet	225ml	Filippo Berio Extra Virgin Olive Oil, extra for drizzling
600ml	whole milk		
6	black peppercorns	2tbsp	freshly chopped flat-leaf parsley
1	bay leaf		
		Sgagliozze to serve	

1 Soak the salt cod in cold water for 24 hours, changing the water every 8 hours. Drain.

2 Place the fish in a saucepan with the milk, peppercorns and bay leaf. Bring to the boil and simmer very gently for about 10 minutes. Take off the heat, cover and leave for another 10 minutes.

3 Remove the fish from the milk and then break it into flakes with a fork or your fingers, removing any skin and bones that remain.

4 Place the fish in a food processor with 2-3 tablespoons of the milk. Pulse until it forms a paste.

5 On a low speed, add the oil little by little as if making mayonnaise. Once the oil is finished, the baccalà should be light and fluffy.

6 Season to taste and leave to cool. Keep in the fridge until ready to serve.

7 Serve on top of the sgagliozze, drizzled with Filippo Berio Extra Virgin Olive Oil and garnished with parsley.

Sgagliozze

Although polenta is not a typical product of Southern Italy, sgagliozze is a signature street food that you can find all year round. The delicacy was born in Bari, but it is prepared throughout Puglia. In essence, it's polenta fried in a square or rectangle, eaten hot. Walking around Bari old town with a hot bag of sgagliozze is one of life's true experiences!

Makes 12 slices

Prep: 5 minutes
Cook: 15 minutes, plus cooling

900 ml	boiling water	200 ml	Filippo Berio Classico Olive Oil, for frying
200 g	express polenta		
1 tsp	salt		

1 Cook polenta according to packet instructions. Spread onto a baking sheet lined with a sheet of baking paper.

2 Place another sheet of baking paper on top, followed by another baking tray. Squeeze together gently to flatten the polenta then place a heavy saucepan on top to weigh it down. Leave to cool completely.

3 Cut the polenta into 12 rectangles, about 4 cm x 8 cm.

4 Pour the Filippo Berio Classico Olive Oil into a large frying pan over a medium-high heat. Fry the polenta pieces, for about 3 minutes each side, until golden brown all over. Drain the polenta pieces on kitchen towel. Season with salt and serve topped with the baccalà mantecato.

Supplí al Telefono

These deep-fried balls are an iconic Roman street food. 'Al telefono' describes the way that, when they are split and pulled apart, the string of mozzarella resembles an old-school telephone cord!

Makes 12

Prep: 20 minutes plus cooling time
Cook: 40 minutes

2 tbsp	Filippo Berio Mild & Light Olive Oil, plus 300 ml for frying	600 ml	beef stock
		2 tbsp	freshly grated parmesan cheese
1	small onion, diced	Salt and freshly ground black pepper	
1	clove garlic, crushed	125 g	mozzarella, cut into 12 sticks about 7 x 3 cm
175 g	minced beef		
100 ml	red wine	2	eggs, beaten
400 g	passata	50 g	plain flour
2 tsp	dried mixed herbs	100 g	dried breadcrumbs
200 g	arborio rice		

1 Heat 2 tbsp Filippo Berio Mild & Light Olive Oil in a large pan, sauté the onions and garlic over a low heat until soft. Stir in the mince and cook until browned.

2 Pour in the wine, reduce by half, then stir in the passata and herbs. Bring to the boil and simmer for 20 minutes, stirring occasionally.

3 Add the rice and cook until it has absorbed most of the passata. Add the beef stock, 100 ml at a time, adding more when the rice has absorbed the liquid. Repeat until the rice is almost ready but a little undercooked (you may not need all the stock). Remove from heat and season to taste.

4 Stir in the parmesan, then spread over a cling film-lined tray to allow the rice to cool quickly. Chill in the fridge until completely cold and set.

5 Divide the rice into 12, place a portion in the palm of your hand. Place a mozzarella stick in the centre and roll the rice in your hands until you have a neat oval shape, making sure the mozzarella is covered by rice. Place on a clean plate and repeat to make the remaining supplí.

6 Place the Filippo Berio Mild & Light Olive Oil in a deep pan or deep-fryer and heat to 170°C.

7 Place the beaten egg in a bowl and the flour and breadcrumbs on plates. Coat the supplí one by one in flour, then egg, and finally in breadcrumbs.

8 Deep-fry the supplí in batches, for 4-5 minutes until golden, then drain on kitchen paper. Serve hot for a molten cheese centre.

Zuppa di Farro

Serves 6

Prep: 15 minutes prep
Cook: 15 minutes, plus cooling

200g	farro, soaked overnight	1	stick celery, finely chopped
200g	dried cannellini beans, soaked overnight (or a 400g tin cannellini beans, drained)	450g	waxy potatoes, peeled and finely chopped
		1	sprig rosemary
4 tbsp	Filippo Berio Classico Olive Oil	4 to 5	fresh sage leaves, roughly chopped
75g	pancetta, chopped	2 litres	vegetable stock, more to taste Salt and freshly ground black pepper
1	onion, finely chopped		
1	carrot, finely chopped	Filippo Berio Extra Virgin Olive Oil, for drizzling	

Farro and bean soup – a very rich and hearty first course from Tuscany. Simple yet nourishing, the soup is enjoyed throughout the winter. Excellent drizzled with Extra Virgin Olive Oil which enhances the flavour of the white beans.

1 Drain the soaked farro and beans. Heat the Filippo Berio Classico Olive Oil in a large saucepan and cook the pancetta for 3-4 minutes, until crisp. Add the onion, carrot and celery and cook over a gentle heat for about 10 minutes, until softened.

2 Stir in the potatoes, farro, beans and herbs. Pour over the stock, then reduce the heat and cover and simmer for about 1 hour, stirring occasionally, or until the beans and farro are very tender and the soup is thick and creamy.

3 Taste and season, then remove from the heat and allow to rest for 10 minutes. Serve with a good drizzle of Filippo Berio Extra Virgin Olive Oil and some crusty bread.

Gnocchetti Sardi alle vongole

Gnocchetti Sardi, also known as Malloreddus, is the foundation of Sardinian cuisine. Accompanied by clams, there's no finer taste in the Mediterranean! The dumplings have tiny ridges and are made simply from semolina, water and saffron. No pasta machine necessary, you can use the back of your fork!

Serves 2

**Prep: 30 minutes plus chilling time
Cook: 15 minutes**

For the gnocchetti		3 tbsp	Filippo Berio Extra Virgin Olive Oil
Pinch	saffron threads		
125 ml	water	1	shallot, finely chopped
200 g	semolina flour (semolato di gran duro)	1	clove garlic, crushed
Pinch of salt		200 ml	passata
For the sauce		12	cherry tomatoes
500 g	fresh clams in shells, cleaned as in vongole recipe		Salt and freshly ground black pepper
		60 ml	vodka
25 g	pancetta		Handful basil leaves

1. Place the saffron threads in the water and leave to infuse for 5 minutes. Place the semolina flour and a good pinch of salt on the work surface and mix together. Make a big hole in the middle and add the saffron water. Using a fork, slowly pull the flour into the water moving around in a circle.

2. When the flour and the water are combined, test it with your fingers. If it sticks to your fingers it's too wet and needs a little more flour. Knead, for about 5 minutes until the dough is elastic. Alternatively, you can do this in a mixer using a dough hook. Wrap the ball in cling film and chill for 30 minutes to relax.

3. Roll the pasta into thin logs, then pinch off small balls. Shape them by pushing against the ridges on the back of a fork or use a gnocchi paddle.

4. To make the sauce, heat the oil in a pan with a lid, add the pancetta and cook until crispy. Reduce the heat and add the shallot and garlic and cook until softened.

5. Stir in the passata and cherry tomatoes, cover and cook until the tomatoes start to burst. Season to taste.

6. Add the clams and pour over the vodka. Increase the heat, cover with the lid, shaking the pan occasionally. When the clams have opened, remove from the heat and discard any clams that haven't opened.

7. Meanwhile bring a pan of water to the boil, add the gnocchetti and cook until it rises to the surface, then remove with a slotted spoon. Add the drained gnocchetti to the clams and sauce and stir to coat.

8. Divide between 2 bowls and serve immediately, garnished with fresh basil.

Spaghetti alle Vongole

This classic Neapolitan dish is one for the purists: packed with flavour, it's best in summer when ingredients are at their freshest. The clams and their briny liquid are the key to the tasty sauce. This dish is traditionally served with the clam shells but you can discard them if you prefer.

Serves 4

Prep: 20 minutes
Cook: 15 minutes

1 kg	fresh clams in shells	½	red chilli, deseeded and finely chopped
350g	dried spaghetti		
		125ml	dry white wine
3 tbsp	Filippo Berio Extra Virgin Olive Oil, plus extra for drizzling	Small bunch flat-leaf parsley, roughly chopped	
		½	lemon, zest and juice
3	cloves garlic, finely chopped		

1   Clean the clams by placing in a bowl of salted, cold water, for 20 minutes, to filter out any sand or grit. Drain.

2   Cook the spaghetti in a large pan of boiling, salted water according to packet instructions, then drain reserving a little cooking water.

3   Meanwhile, heat the Filippo Berio Extra Virgin Olive Oil in a large frying pan, with a lid, reduce the heat and add the garlic and chilli, cook until softened but not browned.

4   Add the clams, then pour over the wine. Increase the heat, cover with the lid, shaking the pan occasionally. When the majority of clams have opened, remove from the heat and discard any that haven't opened.

5   Stir in the drained spaghetti, adding a little of the reserved pasta water if needed, then stir through the parsley, lemon zest and juice.

6   Serve immediately, drizzled with Filippo Berio Extra Virgin Olive Oil.

Here's one of Rome's favourite secondi piatti, Saltimbocca. The name derives from *salti in bocca* – meaning 'jumps in the mouth'. And this is exactly what the flavours will do when you cook this elegant dish! It's usually served with veal, topped with fresh sage and thin slices of prosciutto, but in our version we have used chicken instead. The Roman way is to marinate in wine, but some Italian regions prefer to use oil or saltwater.

Serves 4

Prep: 10 minutes
Cook: 12 minutes

4	small chicken breasts or 2 large, cut in half lengthways	4 tbsp	Filippo Berio Classico Olive Oil
Black pepper, freshly ground		Knob of unsalted butter	
8	sage leaves	100ml	dry white wine
8	slices prosciutto	Lemon wedges, to serve	

1 Place the chicken between two sheets of baking paper and using a rolling pin flatten them to a thickness of 5 mm. Season with black pepper and place 2 sage leaves on each piece

2 Place two slices of prosciutto on each escalope and fold the edges to wrap the chicken.

3 Heat the Filippo Berio Classico Olive Oil in a frying pan and fry 2 escalopes for 2 minutes on each side until coloured and crispy. Transfer from the pan to a plate and cover with foil, repeat with the remaining 2 escalopes. Cover and leave to rest for a few minutes whilst you make the sauce.

4 Return the pan to the heat, add the wine and let it bubble, scraping the pan juice from the bottom of the pan. Add the butter and simmer for 2-3 minutes until you have a sauce.

5 Serve the escalopes with the sauce and crispy rosemary potatoes – and lemon wedges to squeeze over.

Rotolo di Spinaci

Bring the Northern Italian region of Emilia Romagna to your table with these wonderful vegetarian spinach pasta rolls, enriched in tomato sauce. Prepare them in advance, serve and enjoy!

Serves 4-6

Prep: 20 minutes
Cook: about 1 hour

For the tomato sauce

3 tbsp	Filippo Berio Classico Olive Oil
1	onion, finely chopped
2	cloves garlic, crushed sliced
2	400 g cans chopped tomatoes

Salt and freshly ground black pepper

For the filling

800 g	fresh spinach
400 g	ricotta
25 g	parmesan, freshly grated
1	lemon, freshly grated zest

Nutmeg, freshly grated

Handful shredded basil

Salt and freshly ground black pepper

8-10	fresh lasagne sheets
25 g	parmesan cheese, freshly grated

Filippo Berio Extra Virgin Olive Oil, to drizzle

1 Preheat the oven to 180°C, Gas Mark 4.

2 To make the tomato sauce. Heat the Filippo Berio Classico Olive Oil in a large pan and gently cook the onion and garlic for 8-10 minutes until soft but not coloured. Add the tomatoes and season. Bring to the boil; then cover and simmer for 20 minutes, stirring occasionally.

3 Meanwhile make the spinach filling, wilt the spinach in a hot dry pan (do in batches). Once cool enough to handle, squeeze the spinach to remove excess water then roughly chop.

4 In a bowl, mix the spinach with the ricotta, parmesan and basil, then flavour with nutmeg, lemon zest, salt and freshly ground black pepper.

5 Place the lasagne sheets in boiling water to soften slightly, then drain, cover to keep moist.

6 Spread the ricotta filling over each sheet, then roll up from the shorter side, seal with some cold water, making sure the seal is underneath the roll. Cut each roll into 3 x 3 cm rolls.

7 Place the tomato mixture in the bottom of a large gratin dish, place the ricotta rolls on top, drizzle with 1 tbsp Filippo Berio Extra Virgin Olive Oil, then sprinkle over the parmesan.

8 Cover with foil and cook in the oven for 20 minutes, then remove the foil and cook for a further 10 minutes until golden and bubbling.

9 Drizzle with Filippo Berio Extra Virgin Olive oil and serve immediately with a rocket salad.

From Lombardy comes Ossobuco or, literally, 'bone with a hole' – veal shin cut horizontally through the bone exposing the marrow, giving the dish a rich and buttery flavour. Slow cooked, tender and paired with Risotto alla Milanese, this is truly a signature plate.

Serves 4

Prep: 30 minutes
Cook: 2 hours

3 tbsp	Filippo Berio Classico Olive Oil
4	veal shin pieces
2 tbsp	plain flour, seasoned
1	onion, finely chopped
1	carrot, finely chopped
1	stick celery, finely chopped
2	cloves garlic, crushed
3	sage leaves
2	strips unwaxed lemon peel
200 ml	dry white wine
200 ml	chicken stock

For the gremolata

Finely grated zest
1 unwaxed lemon

1	clove garlic, finely chopped
3 tbsp	flat-leaf parsley, freshly chopped

For the risotto Milanese

2 tbsp	Filippo Berio Mild & Light Olive Oil
1	onion, finely chopped
½ tsp	saffron strands
300 g	arborio or carnaroli risotto rice
150 ml	dry white wine
1 litre	fresh vegetable or chicken stock
75 g	freshly grated parmesan cheese

Filippo Berio Extra Virgin Olive Oil, for drizzling

1 Heat a large casserole pot over a high heat and add the Filippo Berio Classico Olive Oil. Place the seasoned flour on a plate and use to dust the veal on both sides.

2 Add the meat to the hot oil and brown well on each side, transfer to a plate. Turn down the heat and add the onion, carrot and celery, cook for 4-5 minutes until softened. Stir in the garlic, sage and lemon peel and cook for 2-3 minutes.

3 Pour in the wine, bring to the boil, then place the veal on top of the vegetables. Pour over the stock and reduce the heat to a simmer. Cover and cook for 1½-2 hrs or until the veal is tender, carefully turning it every 30 minutes.

4 Mix all the ingredients together for the gremolata in a bowl.

5 When the veal is almost cooked, make the risotto Milanese. Heat the Filippo Berio Mild & Light Olive Oil in a wide, non-stick pan over a medium heat. Add the onion and cook, stirring, for 5 minutes, until softened. Stir in the saffron, when it begins to release its colour, add the rice. Stir for 1 minute to coat in the oil, then pour in the wine and bubble until absorbed.

6 Meanwhile, put the stock in a saucepan and keep on a low simmer. Add a ladleful to the rice, stirring until absorbed. Continue adding the stock – 1 ladleful at a time, stirring frequently and making sure it is absorbed before adding the next ladle, until the rice is al dente (about 20 minutes). You may not need all the stock. Stir in the parmesan.

7 Divide the risotto between 4 plates, place the veal shin on top spoon over some of the sauce, then scatter over the gremolata. Drizzle with Filippo Berio Extra Virgin Olive Oil.

Puntarelle alla Romana

Puntarelle is part of the chicory family, grown around Rome, and is traditionally prepared with an anchovy dressing. It is normally served trimmed and soaked, allowing the leaves to relax and soak up the dressing. This recipe also works with chicory. Simply cut 4 heads into thin strips and prepare as directed.

Serves 4 as a side dish

Prep: 20 minutes, plus 1 hour soaking

1	head puntarelle	Juice ½ lemon
For the dressing		75 ml Filippo Berio Extra Virgin Olive oil
1	clove garlic	
2	anchovy fillets	Salt and freshly ground black pepper

1   To prepare the puntarelle, fill a large bowl with cold water and ice cubes and set it aside. Pull the hollow bulbs from the head of puntarelle and strip away the outer leaves, then, using a sharp knife cut each bulb lengthways into thin slices and drop each slice in the iced water. Leave to soak for about an hour during which time they curl up and become crisp.

2   For the dressing, place the garlic, anchovy fillets and a good pinch salt in a mortar and mash with the pestle to a paste. Add the lemon juice to the mix and leave until the anchovy has dissolved.

3   Drain the puntarelle and carefully pat dry or use a salad spinner, place in a bowl.

4   Mash the anchovy mixture again, mix in the Filippo Berio Extra Virgin Olive Oil and season to taste. Pour over the puntarelle, toss to coat, then serve.

The aromatic bulb we know as fennel is popular in Italian cuisine, both raw and cooked. A simple side dish packed with complex flavours, this roasted fennel enlivened with the decadent taste of parmesan and the kick of chilli is an experience to savour.

Serves 4 - 6 as a side dish

Prep: 10 minutes
Cook: about 50 minutes

3 - 4	fennel bulbs, outer leaves removed and fronds reserved	Salt and freshly ground black pepper	
3 tbsp	Filippo Berio Classico Olive Oil	30 g	freshly grated parmesan
2	cloves garlic, crushed	15 g	dried breadcrumbs
2 tsp	fennel seeds, crushed	2 tbsp	flat - leaf parsley, freshly chopped
1 tsp	dried chilli flakes	Filippo Berio Extra Virgin Olive Oil, for drizzling	

1 Preheat the oven to 190°C, gas mark 5. Quarter the fennel bulbs, keeping them intact at the base. Place in a large bowl and toss with the Filippo Berio Classico Olive Oil, garlic, fennel seeds, chilli flakes and seasoning. Put into a large gratin dish or roasting tin and cover tightly with foil.

2 In a small bowl mix together, the parmesan and breadcrumbs. Roughly chop the fronds.

3 Roast for about 30 - 35 minutes, the undersides should be golden. Remove the foil, sprinkle over the reserved fennel fronds and the breadcrumb mixture and return to the oven. Cook for 10 - 15 minutes, or until the fennel is tender and the topping is golden.

4 Sprinkle over the chopped parsley and serve immediately, drizzle with Filippo Berio Extra Virgin Olive Oil.

Berry and Amaretti Semifreddo

This velvety sensation from Naples is a wonderful no-bake dessert, created by folding cream into an Italian meringue. *Semifreddo* translates as 'half cold' which is just how it's served... a creamy slice with fresh fruit on top!

Serves 8-10

Prep: 40 minutes, plus 8 hours freezing time

400g	mixed berries, e.g. raspberries, strawberries, extra to decorate	50g	caster sugar, plus 2 tbsp for step 6
50g	icing sugar	125ml	Filippo Berio Mild Extra Virgin Olive Oil
Finely grated zest and juice 1 unwaxed lemon		400ml	double cream
4	medium eggs, separated	50g	amaretti biscuits, crushed

1   Line the base and sides of a loaf tin (large enough to hold 2 pints of liquid) with baking paper. Quarter the strawberries, put into a pan with the remaining fruit. Add the icing sugar and lemon juice and simmer for 5 minutes, until the berries have softened and the liquid is syrupy.

2   With a slotted spoon, lift out half the berries and set aside. Blend the remaining mixture until smooth and push the purée through a fine sieve into a separate bowl (discard pips). Leave the purée and berries to cool separately.

3   Place the egg yolk, lemon zest and caster sugar in a bowl and beat with an electric whisk for 3-4 minutes until the mixture thickens and is paler in colour. Gradually whisk in the Filippo Berio Mild Extra Virgin Olive Oil.

4   In a separate bowl whisk the cream until it forms soft peaks, then fold into the egg yolk mixture until combined.

5   Fold in the fruit purée and berries.

6   In a clean bowl, whisk the egg whites until they form soft peaks, then whisk in caster sugar 1 tbsp at a time until thick and glossy.

7   Gently fold the egg whites into the berry cream mixture until combined, then gently stir in the crushed amaretti.

8   Pour into the tin and place in the freezer for at least 8 hours.

9   Thaw in the fridge for 1 hour before serving in slices, with extra berries.

Cannoli

These infamous fried pastry tubes, filled with creamy, sweet ricotta cheese are the symbol of Southern Italian culture. They were made even more iconic after being mentioned in 'The Godfather' movie; "Leave the gun. Take the cannoli". Tip: fill the shells just before serving, to avoid the cases getting soggy.

Makes 8-10

Prep: 40 minutes, plus chilling time
Cook: 20 minutes

For the cannoli

150g	plain flour
1 tbsp	caster sugar
Pinch	bicarbonate of soda
1 tsp	ground cinnamon
30g	unsalted butter
1	egg, separated
50ml	dry Marsala or dry white wine
Pinch of salt	
400ml	Filippo Berio Mild & Light Olive Oil

For the filling

350g	ricotta
2 tbsp	icing sugar
1 tbsp	Marsala wine or amaretto
40g	dark chocolate, finely chopped
2 tbsp	candied peel, finely chopped
3 tbsp	pistachios, finely chopped

1 To make the cannoli: place the flour, sugar, bicarbonate and cinnamon into a bowl with a pinch of salt. Add the butter and rub it into the dry ingredients until there are no more lumps. Mix the egg yolk and marsala or wine and add this to the bowl, then mix together and knead to a make smooth dough. Wrap in cling film and rest in the fridge for at least 1 hour.

2 For the filling: place the ricotta, icing sugar and Marsala or amaretto in a bowl and mix together, stir in the chocolate and candied peel. Cover and place in the fridge.

3 Roll out the dough between 2 pieces of baking paper until very thin, using a 11cm cutter, cut out 8-10 circles, wrap these around steel cannoli tubes, sealing the edge with egg white.

4 Pour the Filippo Berio Mild & Light Olive Oil into a deep fat fryer or deep saucepan and heat to 180°C. Fry the cannoli, while on the tubes, a few at a time in the hot oil for about 45-60 seconds until golden brown; the dough will bubble and blister. Carefully take each one out of the oil using tongs and gently shake the cannoli off the tube onto kitchen paper. Allow to cool.

5 When ready to serve, spoon the mixture into a piping bag with a wide nozzle and pipe it into the cannoli. Dip the ends in the pistachios and serve immediately.

Sgroppino

There is nothing better than a refreshing Sgroppino to finish off your meal! This is a centuries old cold mousse cocktail. It was originally a palate cleanser between courses – 'scropin' is the Venetian dialect for 'untying a little knot' – to help digestion during a traditional Italian feast. It is now more common to have as a liquid dessert.

Ingredients per person

1 scoop lemon sorbet	
80 ml	prosecco
1 shot	vodka

1 Place 1 scoop of sorbet into a bowl, add the vodka and mix with a hand mixer, so that it's not too watery.

2 Once mixed, pour in the prosecco.

3 Serve in a flute and garnish with fresh mint.